BRAVE SET STRANGE LAND

*by Donna Foley
illustrated by Ron Mahoney*

Editorial Offices: Glenview, Illinois • Parsippany, New Jersey • New York, New York
Sales Offices: Needham, Massachusetts • Duluth, Georgia • Glenview, Illinois
Coppell, Texas • Ontario, California • Mesa, Arizona

Every effort has been made to secure permission and provide appropriate credit for photographic material. The publisher deeply regrets any omission and pledges to correct errors called to its attention in subsequent editions.

Unless otherwise acknowledged, all photographs are the property of Scott Foresman, a division of Pearson Education.

Photo locators denoted as follows: Top (T), Center (C), Bottom (B), Left (L), Right (R), Background (Bkgd)

Illustrations by Ron Mahoney

10 (C) S. Rubin/The Image Works, Inc., (BL) S. Rubin/The Image Works, Inc.; 12 Stephen Chernin, Stringer/AP/Wide World Photos; 13 Michael Newman/PhotoEdit; 14 (CL) Spencer Platt/Newsmakers/Getty Images, (BL) Jeff Zelevansky/AP/Wide World Photos, (BR) DK Images

ISBN: 0-328-13368-X

Copyright © Pearson Education, Inc.

All Rights Reserved. Printed in the United States of America. This publication is protected by Copyright, and permission should be obtained from the publisher prior to any prohibited reproduction, storage in a retrieval system, or transmission in any form by any means, electronic, mechanical, photocopying, recording, or likewise. For information regarding permission(s), write to: Permissions Department, Scott Foresman, 1900 East Lake Avenue, Glenview, Illinois 60025.

3 4 5 6 7 8 9 10 V0G1 14 13 12 11 10 09 08 07 06

As Tommy, Lisa, and Grandpa stood on the ferry, a voice called out over the loudspeaker. "Welcome to New York Harbor's Ellis Island. Ellis Island was the port of entry for millions of immigrants to America in the late 1800s and early 1900s."

Grandpa had told Tommy and Lisa stories about his grandmother, who came to Ellis Island from Europe. Now they were going to visit the island with him!

Birds were **swooping** and **drifting** through the air above the harbor. Their **glaring** eyes watched the ferry as it passed by. Tommy and Lisa stood by the ferry railing and listened as Grandpa spoke.

"When I was a child my grandmother told me many stories about coming to America," Grandpa said. "She told me about all of the different people who immigrated. They came from many different backgrounds. It was hard for them to leave their homes and come to a strange new land. But they came! They worked hard to make lives in America.

"Most people in the United States have family roots in other parts of the world," Grandpa said. "That's why America has been called a 'melting pot.'

"These days," he added, "immigrants aren't expected to give up their cultures to fit into society as was expected earlier. People are more respectful of immigrants' different traditions. But when my grandmother came to America, she had a hard time. Immigrants faced a lot of prejudice because they were different. They **struggled** to fit in. Can you imagine what it was like?"

"Grandpa, your head is in the clouds," Lisa said with a **giggle.** "Please pay **attention.** It's time to leave the ferry!"

Tommy, Lisa, and Grandpa joined the **looping** line of people. When they reached the bottom of the ferry ramp, Grandpa led them over to a park ranger who was about to start a tour.

"Hello, everyone, and welcome to Ellis Island," said the park ranger. "We start our tour today at the American Immigrant Wall of Honor.

"This wall honors everyone who has immigrated to America through Ellis Island. It also honors people who immigrated through ports in Boston, Philadelphia, Baltimore, San Francisco, Miami, and New Orleans."

The park ranger gave them a moment to think about all of America's immigrants. "Now, let's move on to the main building," he said.

Inside the main building, Tommy looked at the photographs of New York's old immigrant neighborhoods. "It looks so crowded," he said. "There were so many people!"

"Yes," Grandpa replied, "people came from all over the world. My grandmother had neighbors from Russia, Germany, and Ireland. She couldn't talk to most of her neighbors because she didn't speak their languages. For a long time, she couldn't speak English either.

"She never **complained,** but I think she must have been lonely. She must have felt very different."

The park ranger continued speaking. "From 1880 to 1930, twenty-seven million people entered the United States. About twelve million of them came through Ellis Island. Most were from Europe and Canada.

"Immigration slowed down between 1930 and 1965. During those years, many immigrants came from Germany, Canada, Mexico, Britain, Italy, and Latin America. Today, many immigrants to the United States come from Asia and Mexico."

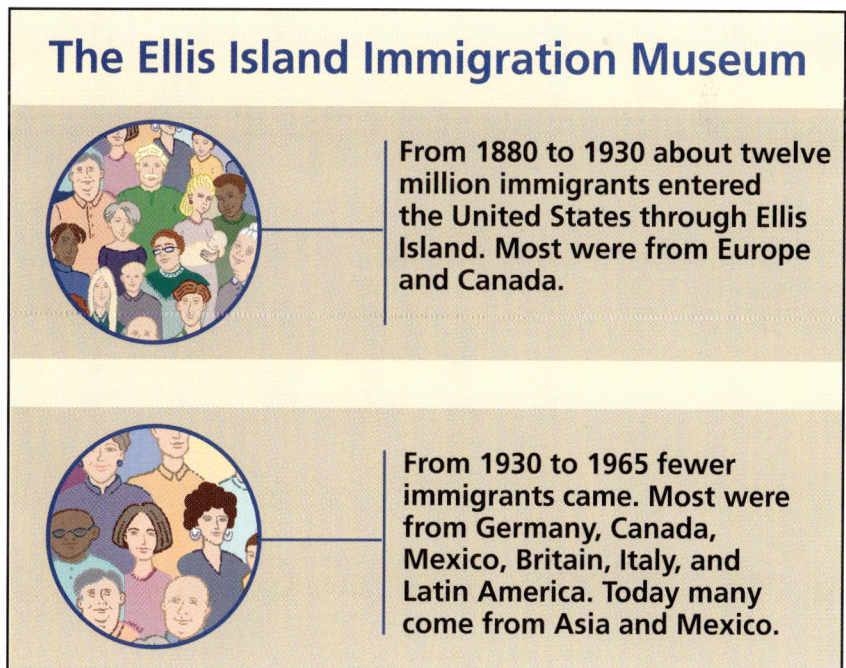

The Ellis Island Immigration Museum

From 1880 to 1930 about twelve million immigrants entered the United States through Ellis Island. Most were from Europe and Canada.

From 1930 to 1965 fewer immigrants came. Most were from Germany, Canada, Mexico, Britain, Italy, and Latin America. Today many come from Asia and Mexico.

Tommy and Lisa looked at more photographs of old immigrant neighborhoods and listened as the park ranger spoke. "The United States is constantly changing," he said. "By 2003 33.5 million U.S. residents had been born in a foreign country! Of those people, about fifty-three percent were from Latin America. Another twenty-five percent were from Asia. America has become a very diverse country!"

"Americans came from everywhere, didn't they, Grandpa?" Lisa asked.

Modern-day families immigrate to the United States.

"They sure did," said Grandpa. "The first Americans were actually the Native Americans. They settled in North America thousands of years before anyone else. Today, people are still coming to America."

"I wonder what it would be like to pick up and leave your home," Lisa said.

"Many immigrants had to work at jobs they'd never worked at before," said Grandpa. "They had to learn to live in new ways. But thanks to all of the brave immigrants who came to America, we have a country rich in different cultures and traditions!"

The park ranger led the tour group into another room. "Now we're in the Great Hall, or registry room," he said. "This is where immigrants waited to be examined. All immigrants had to pass a medical exam. They also needed to show documents in order to enter the United States."

"My grandmother told me about her examination," Grandpa told Tommy and Lisa. "She said that the immigrants were frightened. They were afraid they wouldn't be allowed to enter the United States. Luckily, all went well for her. She wasn't sick, and she had the right papers."

Immigrants were examined in the Great Hall at Ellis Island in New York.

Lisa was thinking about today's immigrants to America. "Where do immigrants enter America today, now that Ellis Island is closed?" she asked the park ranger.

"California is the new Ellis Island," he answered. "It receives most of our country's new immigrants. They come from mainland Asia, the Philippines, Mexico, and Central America. They come by ship, by airplane, and by car."

Today most immigrants enter the United States through the state of California.

The park ranger guided the tour group into a new area. "This is the American Family Immigration History Center," he said. "Here, you can search for your ancestors' records. You can also listen to recordings made by immigrants who entered at Ellis Island. You can even research your family tree if you'd like!"

Lisa turned to Grandpa. "Can we search for Great-Great-Grandmother's records?" she asked.

"That's a wonderful idea!" said Grandpa.

Ellis Island's American Family Immigration History Center has many family records.

"Do you have any more stories about what it was like for her to be an immigrant?" Tommy asked.

"I sure do," said Grandpa. "She always said it was the hardest thing she ever did, and the best thing. Let's start our search by looking for the records of her ship!"

So Lisa, Tommy, and Grandpa spent a happy afternoon in the History Center. They learned about Grandpa's grandmother and the lives of the other brave immigrants who made homes for themselves in a strange new land.

Glossary

attention *n.* careful thinking, looking, or listening.

complained *v.* to have said that you were unhappy, annoyed, or upset about something.

drifting *v.* carrying or being carried along by currents of air or water.

giggle *n.* a silly or uncontrolled laugh.

glaring *adj.* staring angrily.

looping *v.* forming a line, path, or motion shaped so that it crosses itself.

struggled *v.* tried hard; worked hard against difficulties.

swooping *v.* coming down fast on something, as a hawk does when it attacks.